© Aladdin Books Ltd 2001

Designed and produced by
Aladdin Books Ltd
28 Percy Street
London W1P 0LD

First published in
Great Britain in 2001 by
Franklin Watts
96 Leonard Street
London EC2A 4XD

ISBN 0 7496 4163 0
A catalogue record for this
book is available from the
British Library.

Printed in Belgium

Editor
Bibby Whittaker

Literacy Consultant
Phil Whitehead,
Westminster Institute of Education,
Oxford Brookes University

Design
Flick, Book Design and Graphics

Picture Research
Brian Hunter Smart

READING ABOUT

My Home

By Jim Pipe

Aladdin/Watts
London • Sydney

In the city

Hi, I'm Rosa and I live in the city.
My home is in a tall block of flats.

Our flat is on the tenth floor, so I
take the lift to get home.

Taking
the lift

3

There are flats above and below us. Our flat has two bedrooms.

My sister Beth and I share a room. We sleep in bunk beds.

Bunk beds

At night I can see the city lights from the top bunk.

The city is a great place to be!

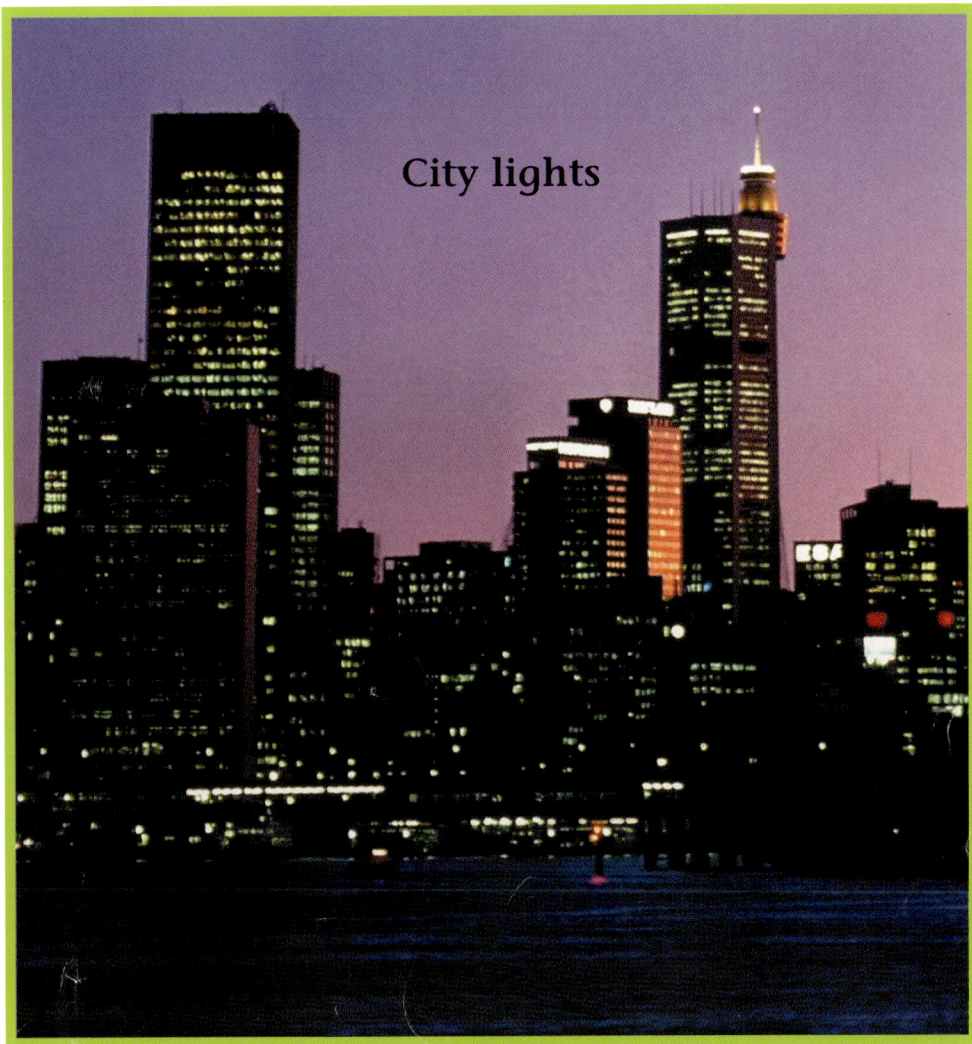

City lights

City people rush here and there.

I like to watch them from the bus.

Sometimes cars get in a jam and
drivers honk their horns.

Bus

In the street

Hi, I'm Jack and I live in the country. It is very quiet here.

From my window I can watch the cows and sheep in the fields.

Window

I can hear birds singing in the
trees at the end of my garden.

Garden

Our home has three bedrooms.
We also have a workshop. We
are making a birdhouse.

Hammer

Nails

Dad cuts the wood with a saw. I rub the wood smooth with sandpaper.

Then Dad knocks in the nails with a hammer.

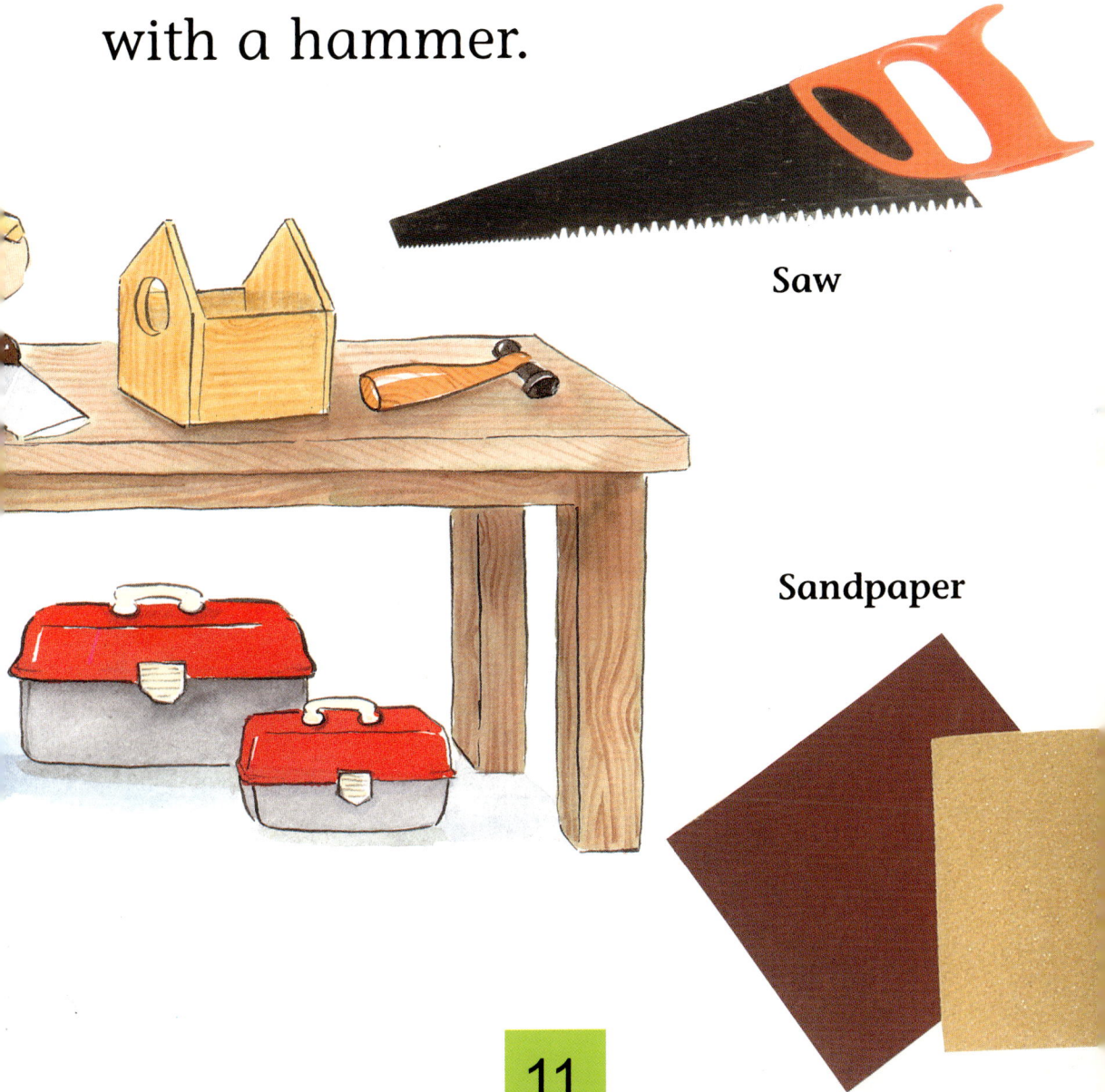

Saw

Sandpaper

11

Our neighbours are the Jacksons. They live across a field.

On their farm they have cows, chickens and pigs.

Farm

Sometimes Mr Jackson lets me sit on his tractor.

The country is a great place to be!

Tractor

Hi, I'm Andy. I live in the suburbs.

The suburbs are on the edge of the city, near to the country.

From my window, I can see
the other houses in my road.

They have trees and bushes
in their gardens.

The suburbs

Our house has three floors. My room is at the top, in the attic.

Attic room

I have to climb a lot of stairs to get to my room.

Sliding down

But I do not have to walk down.

If I am careful, I can slide down!

My friends Joe and Billy live next door.

We love swinging on the rope in Billy's garden.

On the rope

Often we ride our bicycles up
and down the pavement.

Riding bicycles

The suburbs
are the best
place to be!

Rosa, Jack and Andy all think
their home is a great place
to be.

Where do you live?

What do you like
about your home?

Here are some words and phrases from the book.

Swing on a rope

Ride on a bus

Sleep in bunk beds

In the country

Sit on a tractor

Illustrator: Mary Lonsdale at SGA

Picture Credits:
Abbreviations: t-top, m-middle, b-bottom, r-right, l-left, c-centre.
2, 5, 23tr - Corbis. 7, 9, 10 both, 11 both, 12, 14-15, 16, 24
all - Select Pictures. 18, 22tl - Digital Stock.

Did you see these in the book?

Poster

Scooter

Clouds

Carpet

Can you use these words to
write your own story?

Lift

Ride bicycles

Slide down

Live in the city